SEA LIFE: IN AND AROUND THE OCEAN

THE OPEN OCEAN

DAVID AND JULIE LAVENDER

PowerKiDS press

Published in 2027 by The Rosen Publishing Group, Inc.
2544 Clinton Street, Buffalo, NY 14224

First Edition

Editor: Tricia Hoffman
Book Design: Jen Bowers / Beeline Media & Design, Inc.

Photo Credits: Cover, p.1 ©2024 David Keep/Shutterstock.com; cover & throughout book ©2017 Wongymark1/Shutterstock.com; p.4 ©2019 Choksawatdikorn/Shutterstock.com; p.4, p.5 ©2024 Me dia/Shutterstock.com;p.6 ©2017 Andrew Sutton/Shutterstock.com; p.7, p.29 ©2024 Andrea Izzotti/Shutterstock.com; p.7 ©2022 Martin Prochazkacz/Shutterstock.com; p.8, p.9, p.29 ©2023 RLS Photo/Shutterstock.com; p.10, p.11, p.28 ©2018 Onusa Putapitak/Shutterstock.com; p.12 ©2020 NickEvansKZN/Shutterstock.com; p.12 ©2022 John Fader/Shutterstock.com; p.13 ©2017 Maciej Bogusz/Shutterstock.com; p.14, p.15 ©2020 Martin Voeller/Shutterstock.com; p.16 ©2018 Sahara Frost/Shutterstock.com; p.17. ©2013 Arina P Habich/Shutterstock.com; ©2018 Sahara Frost/Shutterstock.com; p.18, p.19 ©2022 Dotted Yeti/Shutterstock.com; p.20, p.28 ©2023 wildestanimal/Shutterstock.com; p.21 ©2007 Stephanie Rousseau/Shutterstock.com; p.22, p.23, p.29 ©2025 FtLaud/Shutterstock.com; p.24 ©Tracey Winholt/Shutterstock.com; p.24 ©2016 Michael Bogner/Shutterstock.com; p.25 ©2017 Tee Wong/Shutterstock.com; p.26, p.27 ©2024 Jonas Gruhlke/Shutterstock.com

Cataloging-in-Publication Data
Names: Lavender, David R., 1961-, author. | Lavender, Julie, author.
Title: The open ocean / by David and Julie Lavender.
Description: Buffalo, New York : PowerKids Press, 2027. | Series: Sea life: in and around the ocean | Includes glossary and index.
Identifiers: ISBN 9781538296059 (pbk.) | ISBN 9781538296066 (library bound) | ISBN 9781538296073 (ebook)
Subjects: LCSH: Marine animals--Juvenile literature. | Marine ecology--Juvenile literature.
Classification: LCC QL122.2 L384 2027 | DDC 591.77--dc23

Publisher's note to educators and parents: Our editors have carefully reviewed these websites to ensure that they are suitable for students. Many websites change frequently, however, and we cannot guarantee that a site's future contents will continue to meet our high standards of quality and educational value. Be advised that students should be closely supervised whenever they access the internet.

Printed in China

CPSIA Compliance Information: Batch #QSPK27. For Further Information contact Rosen Publishing at 1-800-237-9932.

Table of Contents

Far From Land

The open ocean is the deep part of the ocean that lies far from shorelines and coasts. This watery world is full of life. Many small creatures like **plankton**, **krill**, and sardines live in the open ocean. And many predators, some of the largest and fastest animals on the planet, hunt and eat them. In this vast ocean world, it's tough to survive when there's nowhere to hide.

PLANKTON

Blue Whale

Blue whales are the largest animals on the planet. They can grow longer than a basketball court and heavier than 30 elephants! They may live 100 years. Scientists learn this by studying the whale's waxy earplugs.

This endangered species' favorite food is a tiny animal called krill. Blue whales don't even have teeth. They strain krill from the water around them.

Whales are marine mammals, not fish. That means they must surface regularly to breathe air. To breathe in and out, blue whales have two blowholes on top of their head. Whales with teeth, like killer whales and sperm whales, only have one blowhole.

SPERM WHALE

DIVING DEEPER

Blue whales are some of the loudest animals in the world. The underwater sounds they make can be heard by other whales hundreds of miles (km) away.

Lion's Mane Jellyfish

The lion's mane jellyfish may be the largest jellyfish on Earth. The tentacles that hang under its body can grow longer than a blue whale! The stinging cells that cover the tentacles **paralyze** prey with **venom**. Touching a tentacle gives a person a painful sting.

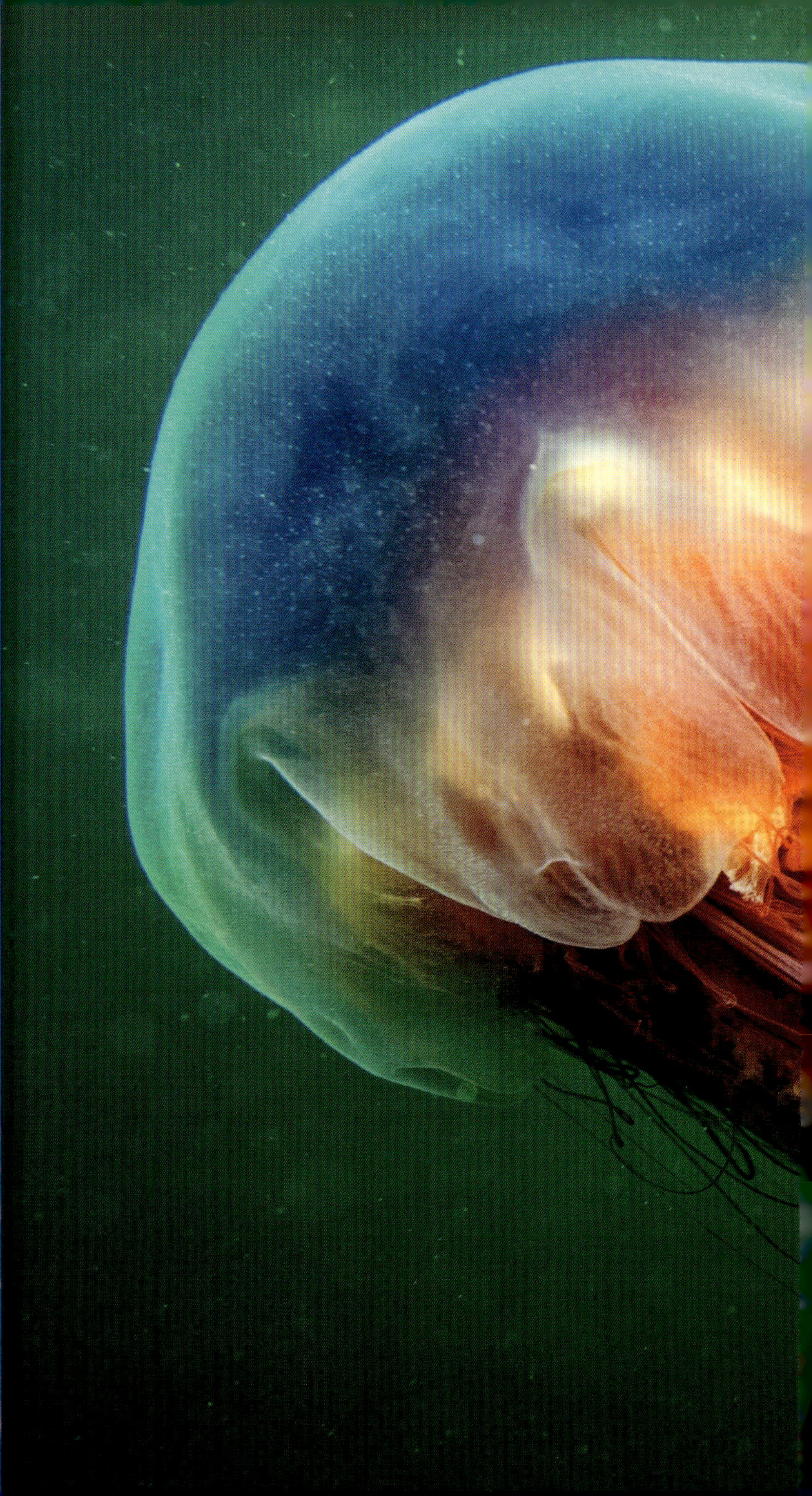

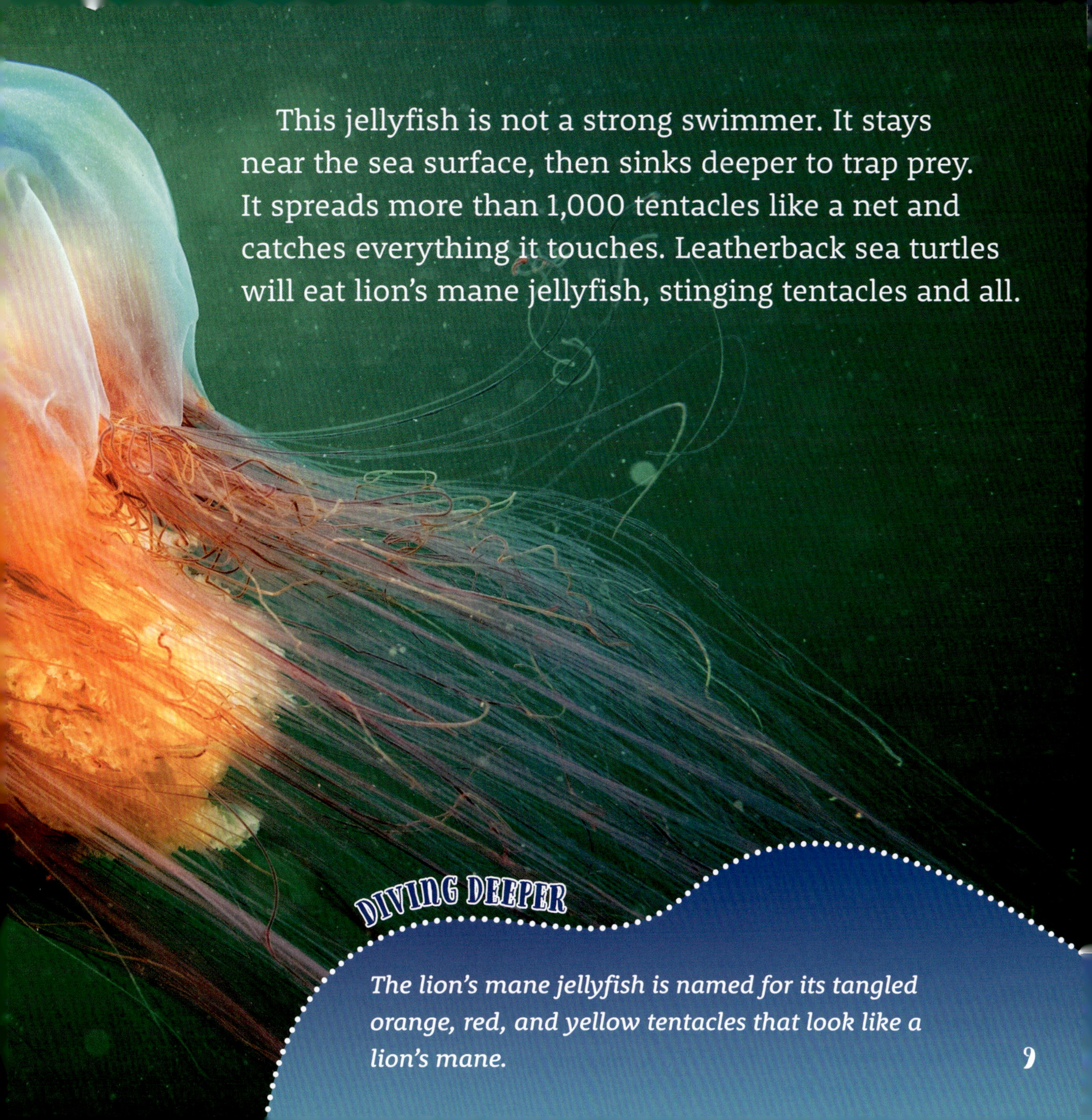

This jellyfish is not a strong swimmer. It stays near the sea surface, then sinks deeper to trap prey. It spreads more than 1,000 tentacles like a net and catches everything it touches. Leatherback sea turtles will eat lion's mane jellyfish, stinging tentacles and all.

DIVING DEEPER

The lion's mane jellyfish is named for its tangled orange, red, and yellow tentacles that look like a lion's mane.

Whale Shark

The biggest fish on Earth is the gentle and slow-moving whale shark. Like other sharks, a whale shark's skeleton is made of **cartilage**, not bone. But unlike other sharks, the whale shark poses no threat to humans. It's longer than a school bus and has a mouth as wide as a teacher's desk, but the giant whale shark feeds on tiny plants and animals called plankton. It can't bite or chew. It swallows its food whole.

Even though it's huge, the whale shark has predators. Killer whales and large sharks like great whites will attack a whale shark. Besides its size, the whale shark's best defense is strong, thick skin that acts like a shield.

DIVING DEEPER

Whale sharks have grayish bodies with pale spots and stripes. Because the pattern of stripes and spots is unique for each shark, scientists can identify individual whale sharks and track them.

Yellow-Bellied Sea Snake

The yellow-bellied sea snake has the largest range of any snake on the planet. It spends its life in the world's warm seas. It is well-suited to life in the open ocean. It has nose openings that can close to keep water out and a flattened tail for swimming.

These snakes hunt fish underwater. They strike and bite when one gets close. Their deadly venom acts quickly. But the sea snake is in no hurry. They can stay underwater without a breath of air for two hours.

DIVING DEEPER

These sea snakes are easy going and rarely aggressive around humans. However, they are highly venomous and their bites can be deadly. If a yellow-bellied sea snake washes ashore, it will not be able to crawl. It is harmless if left alone.

Ocean Sunfish

The heaviest bony fish is the ocean sunfish. It can weigh almost as much as a pickup truck. This huge fish with big eyes and massive fins looks quite strange. It has no tail! Instead, sunfish swim with their fins.

Don't let their size frighten you. Sunfish are harmless, though they sometimes seem curious about divers. Their favorite foods are jellyfish and squid.

DIVING DEEPER

Ocean sunfish can have LOTS of eggs, sometimes as many as 300 million each year. That's more eggs than most creatures produce in a lifetime.

Blue Dragon Sea Slug

The blue dragon is a marine slug that drifts along with ocean currents. It's no bigger than your thumb. It stores an air bubble in its stomach so it can float upside down. That way, its bright blue belly will blend in with the blue water. This provides protection from birds that may want to eat it.

This tiny slug attacks and eats prey bigger than itself, like the venomous Portuguese man o' war. It feeds on the man o' war's tentacles. Then, it steals the man o' war's stinging cells and keeps them to use later! This dragon may not breathe fire, but it packs a painful sting.

PORTUGUESE MAN O'WAR

DIVING DEEPER

Sometimes the wind and ocean currents push blue dragons together in large groups. These groups are called "blue fleets." They may wash up on beaches where they pose a risk to swimmers.

Flying Fish

Spoiler alert! These fish can't truly fly. But they can glide like champs! Flying fish are a popular prey for predators. To escape being eaten, they take to the air.

First, the flying fish swims really fast. It can swim more than 35 miles (56 km) per hour. Then, the fish uses its tail to launch out of the water. It glides above the waves. It uses its fins like wings. It can glide the distance of two football fields.

DIVING DEEPER

Gliding above the water is a unique strategy to escape ocean predators. But attacks can also come from above. Frigate birds often fly over schools of flying fish and wait until they leave the water. When the fish are airborne, they're easy prey for birds.

Leatherback Sea Turtle

Leatherbacks are the world's largest turtles. They grow as long as a kid's surfboard and weigh more than a ton (907 kg)! Their name comes from their shells. Most turtles have a very hard shell covered in scales. The leatherback's shell feels rubbery. It is covered with a layer of skin that looks and feels like leather.

Male leatherbacks never leave the ocean after hatching and crawling to the surf. They spend their lives swimming and eating jellyfish. Female leatherbacks leave the ocean briefly during nesting season. They crawl onto a beach to lay their eggs in the sand.

DIVING DEEPER

The warmth of the sand in a leatherback's nest determines if the young turtles will be male or female. Sand around 85 degrees Fahrenheit (30 degrees Celsius) results in males and females. Hotter sand means all ***hatchlings*** *will be female. Cooler sand produces all male hatchlings.*

Sailfish

Imagine you are one of the fastest fish in the sea. You have a large fin that looks like a sail. You use it to push the small fish you eat where you want them. And you have a spear sticking out of your face! You hit the small fish with it. Bang. Slash. Stab. Then, you gobble them up. This is the life of a sailfish.

The fin that looks like a boat's sail is where these fish get their name. The mouthpart that looks like a spear is called a bill. They are part of the billfish family, which also includes marlin and swordfish.

DIVING DEEPER

Sailfish change their skin colors based on their moods. When excited, they may become bright blue or purple. When they attack prey, their skin color gets darker.

Remora

Remoras attach to larger animals using a special fin. The fin works like a **suction cup**. Remoras are known to ride along on sharks, whales, manta rays, and sea turtles.

Remoras do not harm the host fish they attach to. In fact, they can benefit the host by cleaning it of **parasites**. When it is time to eat, remoras let go of their host by relaxing their muscles.

DIVING DEEPER

Fishermen around the world use remoras like live bait. They tie a line to the remora's tail and release it in the water. The remora finds a big fish to stick to. Then, the fisherman can catch both the remora and its host.

Life in the Open Ocean

The open ocean is huge beyond imagination. It is very wide and very deep. Blue water and rolling waves as far as the eye can see. Many of the sea creatures that call this watery world home will live their entire lives without ever seeing land. This is life in the open ocean.

Who Am I?

Can you guess which open ocean creature is shown in each zoomed-in photo? Look closely at these images and use the clues to help you figure it out. Then, check your answers below. How many did you get right?

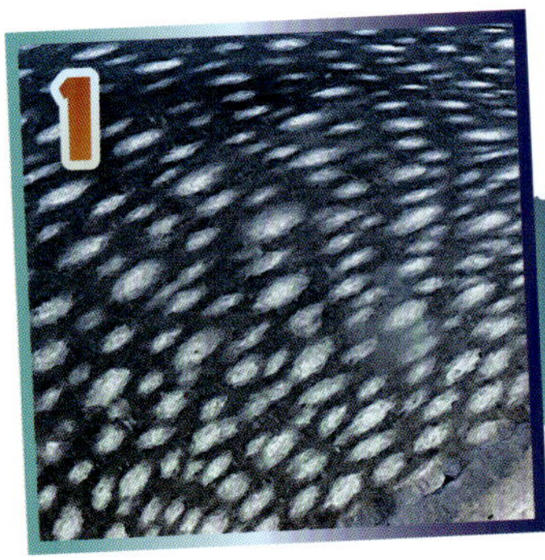

- *I eat lots of plankton.*
- *My thick skin protects me.*
- *My skeleton is made of cartilage.*

- *My shell feels like leather.*
- *I like to eat jellyfish.*
- *I'm the world's biggest turtle.*

- *I am a marine mammal.*
- *I can make very loud sounds underwater.*
- *I am the largest animal on Earth.*

- *My nose is a long spear called a bill.*
- *I am one of the fastest fish in the sea.*
- *My top fin looks like a boat's sail.*

- *I am not a strong swimmer.*
- *I have very long tentacles.*
- *I am the largest jellyfish in the ocean.*

1. whale shark; 2. leatherback sea turtle; 3. blue whale; 4. sailfish; 5. lion's mane jellyfish

Glossary

cartilage (KAHR-tuh-lij): a tough, flexible material that provides support like bone, but is not as hard as bone

hatchlings (HACH-lingz): very young animals that have just hatched from an egg

krill (KRIL): tiny shrimplike creatures that live in the ocean and are an important food source for many animals

paralyze (PAR-uh-lize): to make an animal helpless or unable to move

parasites (PAR-uh-sites): an animal that lives on or inside another living thing

plankton (PLANGK-tuhn): tiny animals and plants that drift or float in oceans and play a very big role in the ocean's food chain

suction cup (SUHK-shuhn kuhp): a cupped object that sticks to smooth surfaces

venom (VEN-uhm): a toxic liquid used by some animals against prey or an enemy

Fact Check

1. A whale shark's skeleton is made of ________.
   a. bone   b. cartilage   c. shell
2. The body of the ocean sunfish looks strange because it has no ________.
   a. eyes   b. fins   c. tail
3. Leatherback sea turtles get their name from their ________.
   a. shell   b. eggs   c. scales

Answers: 1. b, 2. c, 3. a

Further Reading

Bodden, Valerie. *Amazing Animals: Sharks.* The Creative Company, 2022.
Bolte, Mari. *I Am Not an Octopus: Animals in the Ocean.* Pebble, 2022.
Lavender, Julie and David. *Shark Watch: What's for Lunch?* Mitchell Lane Publishers, 2026.

On the Internet

Ocean at Home
www.whoi.edu/ocean-at-home/
Enjoy online learning activities that include virtual ocean encounters, coloring pages, maps, and more.

Ocean Channel
www.marinebio.org/creatures/gallery/
Watch marine life, science, and conservation videos from around the world.

Marine Biology
www.amnh.org/explore/ology/marine-biology#hands-on
Learn about marine biology with games, reading, hands-on activities, and videos.

Index

About the Authors

David and Julie Lavender love visiting beaches and looking for sea creatures. They like to look for shark's teeth that wash up on the beach too. David worked as an entomologist and a wildlife biologist. Julie taught school kids and homeschooled the couple's four children. Julie and David write books together to encourage kids to celebrate the wonder of nature around them. They love reading lots of books to their three grandchildren.